spatial murmuring

Published in Great Britain in 2012 by
Papadakis Publisher

An imprint of New Architecture Group Limited

Kimber Studio, Winterbourne, Berkshire, RG20 8AN, UK

Tel. +44 (0) 1635 24 88 33
info@papadakis.net
www.papadakis.net

Publishing Director: Alexandra Papadakis
Design: He.Lo Architects LLP, Alexandra Papadakis
Production Assistant: Juliana Kassianos
Intern: Ian Caswell

Concept: Sónia Nunes Henriques and Jan-Maurits Loecke
Front cover: "Spatial Murmuring" Kuwait 2011, © Jan-Maurits Loecke
All "Mapping" hand drawings © Jan-Maurits Loecke and Sónia Nunes Henriques
Drawings on pages 28-31 © Álvaro Siza Vieira

ISBN 978 1 906506 28 5

Published with the support of the British Council

Printed and bound in China

The authors would like to thank all contributors and the team at Papadakis Publisher. Thanks also to the following, whose collaboration and support have proved invaluable in the making of this book: Paul Virilio for les étoiles; Hildegard for her constant support; Malcolm Spencer and Squareleg for their pearls of wisdom; Kristin Freireiss and Hans-Jürgen Commerell for their encouragement at the start; Jens Jansen for giving us a good push; Scott Radcliffe; João Ornelas for playing his music in the final phase.

Sónia Nunes Henriques
Jan-Maurits Loecke

spatial murmuring

migration of spaces and ideas

a conversation: Hans-Ulrich Obrist, Saskia Sassen, Richard Parkinson, Álvaro Siza Vieira, Aaron Betsky, Ricky Burdett, Hildegard Weber, Beatrice Galilee, Wilhelm Bruck, Rita Kersting, Michael Jansen, Oscar Niemeyer, Paulo Sergio Niemeyer, Victoria Bell, Marcus Altfeld

 PAPADAKIS

CONTENTS

for Maximus

New York

Cairo

Thessaloniki

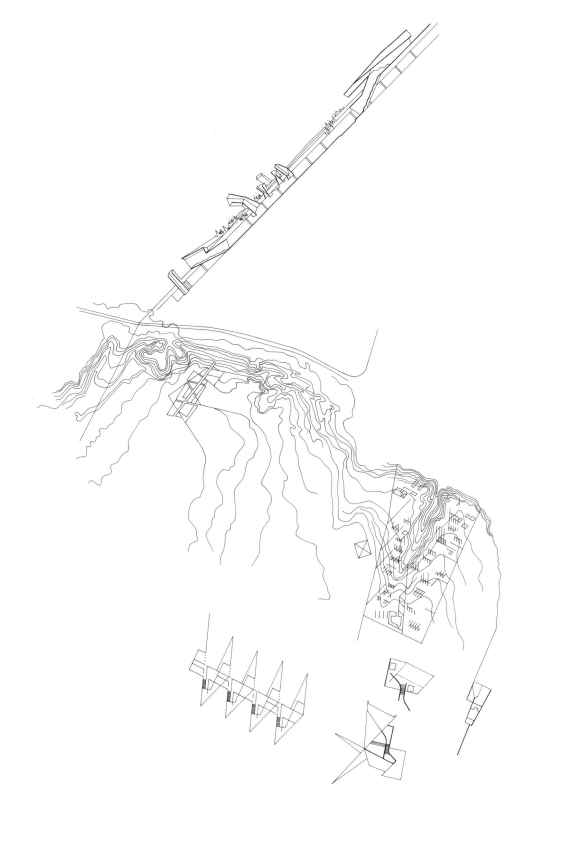

EAR & SPACES
Wilhelm Bruck

Sitting on the slopes of semi-circular valley basins, our ancestors would have heard the cry of beasts and the song of birds, would have listened to the humming of bees, the wind in the trees, perceived the activities of Pan and the nymphs, and sensed the all encompassing spatial murmuring.

Did not such acoustic experiences first lead to the idea of the amphitheatre? Are not the grottos with their echoes and resounding caves the ancestors of our mosques and cathedrals? And was not language already set on stage in Delphi? It would be exciting to show how the theatrical, declamatory, demagogic and artistic potential of language and music were revealed against the backdrop of the architectural development of public spaces, and there flourished in the most astounding forms of expression.

Our experience of sound is tied to spaces, both concrete and imaginary ones. But we cannot perceive space itself through the eye alone, which separates subject and object; we partake in it via the ear which joins in a binding way and transfers the outside to the inside. Is it after all not the first cry of the wild geese but the silent V-formation on their flight south which evokes the idea of a quasi infinite space (and at the same time an infinite yearning)?

What is true of space is also true for our environment and, not least, for our fellow human beings. How can we get to know them better than by listening to them? "Choose your wife with the ear, not with the eye!", says an old proverb. It is primarily our sense of hearing which creates a relationship between ourselves and others.

Rational relations of whole numbers, which are the basis for the harmonies of well formed spaces and compositions, are being measured by the ear in the process of hearing, while the miracle of proportions remains intact. According to Jakob v. Uexküll the ear is the central switchboard for the sense of space and time, and for their transition to infinity. Who could separate and define the inexhaustible mix of countless physical, psychological and spiritual processes which merge into one single experience, especially while we listen to "grande musique" in magnificent spaces? Such experiences are still most aptly described by the explanations used in modern physics to characterise the new conception of the world, which poets and wise men have formulated again and again for centuries: We are participants in an immense, complete and fluid system, in which everything resonates and constantly interacts, in which spirit and energy, gravity and matter change into one another, and we find ourselves "outside of a reality which we call time." (David Bohm)

However, it does not necessarily require large dimensions to step out of time, to experience time as presence, and the moment as eternity. "In fact the least, the faintest, the lightest, the rustling of a lizard, a breath, a whoosh, a glimpse - little is needed for true happiness. Hark! ("Das Wenigste gerade, das Leiseste, Leichteste, einer Eidechse Rascheln, ein Hauch, ein Husch, ein Augen-Blick - Wenig macht die Art des rechten Glücks. Still!") (Friedrich Nietzsche in *Also sprach Zarathustra*). If only it is silent enough inside and all around us, then we can listen "with the ears of the soul" (Rumi) to the "harmony of the spheres", which is the "background radiation" of all art.

Let us therefore protect and create 'spaces for listening' within us which are free from the well trodden paths of materialistic and mechanistic thought with its highly developed art of separation. Let us open spaces within us which are free from the egoistic, purpose-driven actionism that can be so destructive for the community; let us learn to be more perceptive once again, and listen to the harmonies (Zusammenklänge).

Let us also protect and create "spaces of listening" in our living environments and cityscapes. These are not areas of withdrawal, in which we close our ears and search for the unbearable "silence" of soundless space. No, on the contrary! They are open spaces which are not contaminated by noise, but instead flooded with pulsating life. They are meeting places where we don't envy our neighbour's territory, but where everyone can breathe freely and unfold their potential, thereby functioning as catalysts in our cities.

The range of possibilities for the construction of such "spaces for listening" (Hör-Räume) is inexhaustible. I can instantly think of two completely different examples: the first, both well known and exemplary, is the Guggenheim Museum in Bilbao, which I remember with unbridled enthusiasm. Being so famous it does not need any description. The other is constituted by several interconnected streets in the centre of Mexico City, which used to carry heavy traffic. Thanks to some very simple, modest improvements they have undergone a convincing metamorphosis in the past few years. They have been closed to motorised traffic, no shopping malls or tourist attractions have been built, the pubs and bars have remained modest, tables and benches have been placed in the middle of the streets, lawns and trees protected, and a parking space transformed into a kids' playground. How beautiful!

Here spaces of communication have been created where we can listen to and understand one another, even without raising our voices; where we have the opportunity to perceive complex connections, to listen to the questions of our fellow human beings, of the arts or the environment - however hard they might be to decipher at times - and to look for answers. And if we are blessed we might perceive that spatial murmuring and, in the words of R.M. Rilke, "the unbroken news which is created by silence" ("die ununterbrochene Nachricht, die aus der Stille sich bildet").

Ceuta

Bonn

Palisades Glacier

Berlin

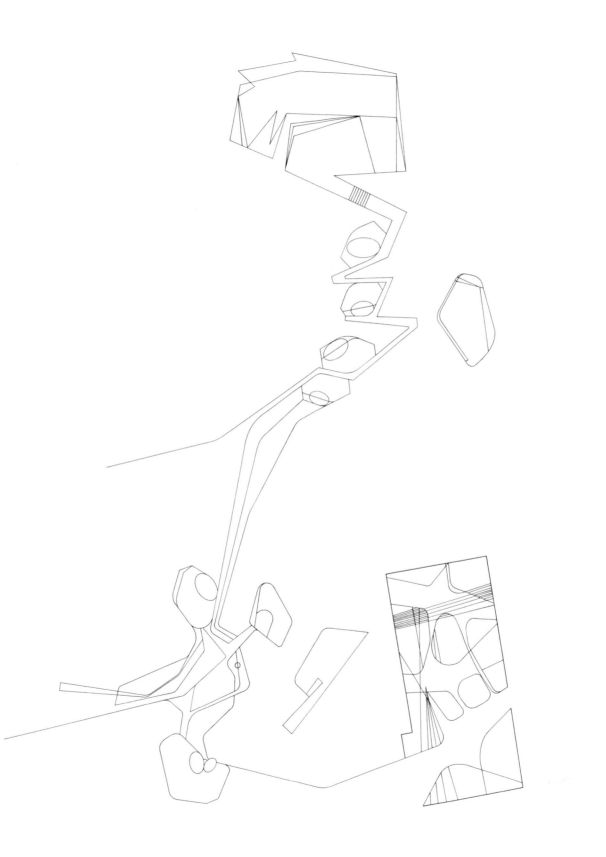

THE GLOBAL STREET
Saskia Sassen

The uprisings in the Arab world, the daily neighborhood protests in China's major cities, Latin America's piqueteros and poor people demonstrating with pots and pans - all are vehicles for making social and political claims. We can add to these the very familiar anti-gentrification struggles and demonstrations against police brutality in U.S. cities during the 1980s and in cities worldwide in the 1990s and continuing today. Most recently, the over 100,000 people marching in Tel Aviv, a first for this city, not to bring down the government, but to ask for access to housing and jobs; part of the demonstration is Tel Aviv's tent city, housing mostly impoverished middle-class citizens. The *Indignados* in Spain have been demonstrating peacefully throughout the country, but most visibly in Madrid and Barcelona, for jobs and social services. Similar demands guided the 600,000 who took to the streets in late August in several cities in Chile. The "riots" in London in August 2011 and the Occupy movement in the United States, all respond to social questions.

These are among the diverse instances that together make me think of a concept that takes it beyond the empirics of each case - The Global Street. It is not new; indeed, the global street is part of many of our histories across time and space, even as its specific forms vary accordingly. In each of the current cases, I would argue that the street, the urban street, as public space is to be differentiated from the classic European notion of the more ritualized spaces for public activity, with the piazza and the boulevard the emblematic European instances. I think of the space of "the street", which of course includes squares and any available open space, as a rawer and less ritualized space. The Street can, thus, be conceived as a space where new forms of the social and the political can be made, rather than as a space for enacting ritualized routines. With some conceptual stretching, we might say that politically, "street and square" are marked differently from "boulevard and piazza": the first signals action and the second, rituals.

Seen in this way, there is an epochal quality to the current wave of street protests, despite their enormous differences from the extraordinary courage and determination of protesters in Syria to the flash crowds convoked via social media to invade a commercial street block for ten minutes that we have seen in cities in the United States, the United Kingdom, and Chile.

In what follows I position these specifics in a larger conceptual frame: the focus is on dimensions of these diverse politics that have at least one strategic moment in the space that is the street – the urban street, not the rural or suburban street. The city is the larger space that enables some of this and also the lens that allows us to capture the history-making qualities of these protests. The larger background for these protests is a sharp slide into inequalities, expulsions from places and livelihoods, corrupt political classes, unfettered greed, and in the most significant of these struggles, extreme oppression – trends documented in detail elsewhere. (*Globalizations* 2010).

The Social Physics of the City

The city is a space where the powerless can make history. That is not to say it is the only space, but it is certainly a critical one. Becoming present, visible, to each other can alter the character of powerlessness. I make a distinction (Sassen 2008, chaps. 6 and 8) between different types of powerlessness. Powerlessness is not simply an absolute condition that can be flattened into the absence of power. Under certain conditions powerlessness can become complex, by which I mean that it contains the possibility of making the political, or making the civic, or making history. There is a difference between powerlessness and invisibility/impotence. Many of the protest movements we have seen in North Africa and the Middle East are cases in point: these protesters may not have gained power, they are still powerless, but they are making history and politics. This then leads me to a second distinction, which contains a critique of the common notion that if something good happens to the powerless it signals empowerment. The notion that powerlessness can become complex can be used to characterize a condition that is not quite empowerment. Powerlessness can be complex even if there is no empowerment.

What is being engendered in the 2011 uprisings in the cities of the MENA region, Spain, Greece, the US, and others, is quite different from what it might have been in the medieval city of Weber. Weber identifies a set of practices that allowed the burghers to set up systems for owning and protecting property against more powerful actors, such as the king and the church, and to implement various immunities against despots of all sorts. Today's political practices, I would argue, have to do with the production of "presence" by those without power, and with a politics that claims rights to the city and to the country rather than protection of property. What the two situations share is the notion that through these practices new forms of the political (for Weber, citizenship) are being constituted and that the city is a key site for this type of political work. The city is, in turn, partly constituted through these dynamics. Far more so than in a peaceful and harmonious suburb, the contested city is where the civic is made (Sassen 2008, chap. 6).

We see this potential for the making of the civic across the centuries. Historically the overcoming of urban conflicts has often been the source for an expanded civicness. The cases that have become iconic in western historiography are Augsburg and Moorish Spain. In both, a genuinely enlightened leadership and citizenry worked at constituting a shared civicness. But there are many other both old and new cases. Old Jerusalem's bazaar was a space of commercial and religious coexistence for long periods of time. Istanbul, Shanghai, Bombay, just to mention a few, each saw periods of extraordinary mixes of religion, culture, ethnicity, and significant inflows of people from diverse countries, where the daily negotiations of difference contributed to the urbanity and cosmopolitanism of these cities. Outsiders in Europe's cities, notably immigrants, have experienced persecution for centuries; yet in many a case their successful claims for inclusion had the effect of expanding and strengthening the rights of citizens as well.

In its own specific forms, this capacity to override old hatreds or mere indifference, became evident in the multiple uprisings of 2011. Tahrir Square has become the iconic case, partly because key features of the process became visible as they stretched over time: the discipline of the protesters, the mechanisms for communicating, the vast diversity of ages, politics, religions, cultures, and the struggle's extraordinary trajectory. But in fact we now know that these features are also at work in other protest sites, often in obscure ways. In Yemen's Saana, conflicting tribes found a way to coalesce with each other and with the protesters against the existing regime in a matter of weeks. These are just two instances of how urban space can hold together differences and enable the constituting of a system of trust, albeit precarious trust, around a shared objective. This is not a minor achievement.

The conditions and the mechanisms are specific to each of the 2011 uprisings. Yet in all these cases overcoming old conflicts and inherited differences became the source for an expanded civicness. This is not urban *per se*, but the conflicts and the civicness assume particularly strong, legible forms in major cities. Further, we see an enabling of the powerless: urban space makes their powerlessness complex, and in that complexity lies the possibility of making the political, making the civic.

The Limits of Powerful Communication Technologies

Beyond complex questions of norms, the city also makes visible both the limits and the unrealized potential of communication technologies such as Facebook. Much has been written and debated about its role in the Egyptian mobilizing in Tahrir Square and protest organizing. In the US, there was much debate on the notion of a "Facebook revolution" signalling that the protest movement was, at the limit, a function of communication technologies, notably social media. It seems to me a common type of conflation of a technology's capacities with a massive on-the-ground process that used the technology. In my research (Sassen 2008, chap. 7; Latham and Sassen, 2005) I find that this type of conflation results from a confusion between the logic of the technology as designed by the engineer and the logic of the users. The two are not one and the same. The technical properties of electronic interactive domains deliver their utility through complex ecologies that include (a) non-technological variables, notably the social, the subjective, the political, material topographies, and so on, and (b) the particular cultures of use of different actors.

Thus, Facebook can be a factor in very diverse collective events – a flash mob, a friends' party, the uprising at Tahrir Square. But that is not the same as saying that they are all achieved through Facebook. As we now know, if anything Al Jazeera was a more significant medium, and the network of mosques was the foundational communication network in the case of the Tahrir Square Friday mobilizations.

One synthetic image we can use is that these larger ecologies are partly shaped by the particular logic embedded in diverse domains. When we look at electronic interactive domains as part of these larger ecologies, rather than as a purely technical condition, we make conceptual and empirical room for the broad range of social logics driving users, and the diverse cultures of use through which these technologies are used. Each of these logics and cultures of use activates an ecology or is activated by it. The effect of taking this perspective is to position Facebook in a much larger world than the thing itself (Sassen, 2012). In this way, we focus on the minimalist version of Facebook: the larger ecology within which a Facebook action is situated rather than the 'world of Facebook' with its billion subscribers. But the protest movement in Tahrir Square also shows us a second aspect of these new technologies: the fact of a new ecology in the use of Facebook and other such social media. This makes visible both the limits of the current format and the capacity of collective action in the city to inscribe a technology. Facebook space itself is today mostly described by experts as part of social life for a large majority of its subscribers. But the network capability involved clearly cannot be confined to this function. The shifts that become visible when we take into account the types of ecologies mobilized, rather point to a far larger range of uses/practices. The Tahrir Square protest movement embodies these shifts and relations. In Tahrir Square Facebook space is not "social life". Rather, it is more akin to a tool.

The potential of digital media for immobile or place-centred activists concerned with local, not global, issues points to the making of larger ecologies that will be different from the ecologies of globally oriented users. For instance, the fact that specific types of local issues (jobs, oppression) recur in localities across the world that engage local, immobile activists in each place, can generate a kind of globality that does not consist of, or depend on, them communicating. This is also a feature of the 2011 Arab uprisings — a recurrence of protests in very diverse places in the region that do not depend on direct communication across these different places, and yet, all together make for a larger and more complex formation than each individual struggle (Sassen, 2008, chap. 7).

This points to a kind of imaginary situation where the actual communications are a third point in a triangle — they are part of the enabling ecology of conditions but that ecology is not simply about communication among participants as is the case in so much Facebook activity. It invites us to ask: how can the new social media add to functions that go beyond mere communication and thereby contribute to a more complex and powerful condition/capability?

Conclusion: THE CITY: Its return as a lens onto major world events

The city has long been a site for the exploration of many major subjects confronting society. But it has not always been a heuristic space — a space capable of producing knowledge about some of the major transformations of an epoch. This was the case in the first half of the twentieth century. And it is so in today's global era. The city has once again emerged as a strategic site for understanding some of the major new trends reconfiguring the social order. The city and the metropolitan region are one location where major macro and global trends, even when not urban, materialize; it is, then, a space that can give us knowledge about developments that are not urban *per se*. The city might be just one moment in what can be complex multi-sited trajectories, but it is a strategic moment.

[1] This is based on "The Global Street: Making the Political", *Globalizations*, October 2011, Vol. 8, No. 5, pp. 565–571

References
- Globalizations. (February/April 2010). Globalization and the Financial Crisis, (Special Issue) Vol 7 (nrs1-2).
- Latham, Robert and Saskia Sassen, eds. (2005) Digital Formations: IT and the New Architectures in the Global Realm (New York: Princeton University Press).
- Leistert, Oliver and Theo Röhle, eds. (2011) Generation Facebook. Germany: Transcript Verlag.
- Sassen, Saskia. (2012) "Interactions of the Technical and the Social: Digital Formations of the Powerful and the Powerless." Information, Communication & Society. DOI:10.1080/1369118X.2012.667912.
- (2010). "When the City Itself Becomes a Technology of War." Theory, Culture &Society, 27(6), pp. 33-50.
- (2008). Territory, Authority, Rights:From Medieval to Global Assemblages (Princeton, NJ: Princeton University Press)

New York

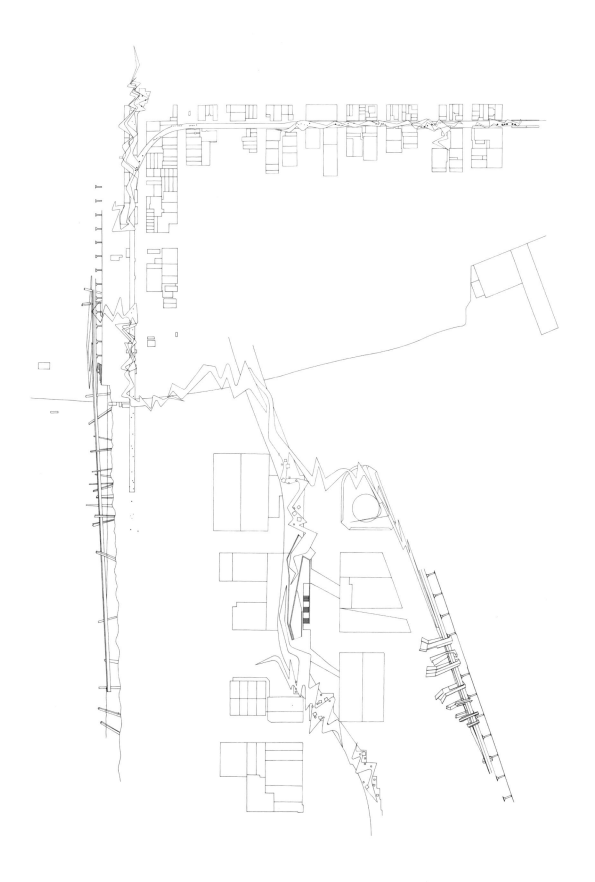

ISLANDS

Hans Ulrich Obrist, in conversation with Cedric Price

HUO – You mentioned before that it is not enough to solve the problem, there must be more.

CP – That's right, I think it's essential that we delineate the problems, as Juan [Herreros] has done in his notes. But we must build on those problems to stop architecture and planning being problem based, and making them opportunity-based for improvement, for the better. That is the basis of how we look at the country, not in its physical sense, but at its population, both existing and future. There are lots of people in England and Germany whose minds are vaguely around Majorca in relation to having a holiday in the future. But we step in; we want to advantage them, while in no way isolating the existing population, but showing that the existing population can find an advantage from all these blasted foreigners having their holidays there all the time. So it's a positive thing – in both instances.

HUO – That's interesting, because what obviously comes to my mind is your New York competition entry, where this problem was also an issue; but you didn't add anything, you were actually subtracting. Maybe in a similar way one could think about subtraction in this case.

CP – Yes, it's rather like that. The whole business about "The good thing about you being there". I've been there once, many years ago.

HUO – When was that?

CP – I forget the date, but in the mid-sixties, I think. It was very, very hot. That's what I remember; not the beauty, not the beaches. I just remember the heat. Now that could be an advantage in itself. Not lovely brown German bodies sitting in the sun, but what does the sun, which is always there, cause in relation to, say, trees, olives?

HUO – Cedric, you mentioned the advantages of islands?

CP – In the past we tended to keep prisoners on islands, that is, we tended to put people there that we didn't want to see again. But there is an advantage in islands. Holidaymakers know the advantages: they seem to be called sun and cheap food. But we must do more than that. We must transcend the centuries from the prisoners on the islands, and immigrants. To what else? Holidaymaking isn't sufficient. The people who live there haven't been touched; or rather, they have been touched, but adversely up until now. So we need a positive consideration.

[after some delay]

CP – This is a period of real enjoyment, matter of fact, one can revise one's parts one and two [of this interview]. And this is the value of delays. The advantage of silence and doubt, and the broken pencil, or it's equivalent, the smashed equipment: you need a moment to sharpen the pencil, or the equivalent for your imagination, new tapes or new batteries. So the advantage of silence starts now! [laughs and stops talking] It's the advantage of being incomplete.

HUO – You mentioned *Venic*.

CP – *Venic* is based on my non-scheme for Venice, which completed itself, and therefore Venic was the job title.

HUO – So the non-scheme for the island you are developing here will also be incomplete?

CP – It will have to be. Unless there are tidal waves in the Mediterranean, which haven't been planned yet. The future of the island, of any island, should always be incomplete. And there's no answer to a useful island apart from a tidal wave, but that's a bit disastrous. Apart from that, the continuous ebb and flow of the tide which delineates the island is in itself a change of conditions, which should be put to some advantage. I've just handed you the geological map of the island. There is something about this particular island, because it's very popular with English and German holidaymakers. So it's false in one way because in the other way they depend on the tourism for their economy. It's an imbalanced economy, but it might always be imbalanced. It might be one of the ways you assist islands or land with a lot of water around it, like Florida has a lot of water around it, and this business about water and free time is a source of false economy, and the economy of tourism. It's an annual economy. They spend money, but on a seasonal basis, because of the weather or the soil or the beaches. So tourism is not a false economy, but a different kind of economy, and we feel that countries should have an economy that supports them all year round.

HUO – That brings us to the question of time and the distortion of time.

CP – Yes. Previously, the distortion of time in relation to this Spanish island was because of the rich. Churchill used to stay there.

Money buys time. Free time is rich people's time. And if we are all in some way related to the rest of the globe on holiday, the Western world is unnaturally rich. Then it might be the indicator of what future islands might do. It's distortion of time relative to a particular area?. So it becomes like heroic materialism, in a way. Materialism isn't bad. Unlike a lot of capitalism, which I personally find rather revolting, because I'm biased, but materialism doesn't need to be. But it needs distortion of time resulting in the advantage that you can take of a particular area, an island, by assessing its geological [character], its seasons, its nasty weather, its accessibility. In mid-winter fewer people want to go to Florida, although people still live there. You find English footballers signed to Madrid who have a place in Florida. That's a distortion of time that money can feed. If we are trying to increase the availability of money as a particular currency of time – the availability of money makes you more of a well-heeled nomad — then that must apply to any sort of island. Why do the Germans or the British love holidaying in Majorca? They have a long way to go. This is the mystery of the problem, but I don't think we have a problem; it's just that we don't realize it has to do with the new freedom of time, which probably should be aligned to availability of money. If we don't like our money system, and the provision of good health or long life is related to money, it should be related to money, so that ownership of wealth is a halfway stage in what we're talking about. It's imperfect to have to have wealth in order to have good conditions. That's the interesting thing about the National Health Service in the United Kingdom; It's one of the largest businesses in Europe! I've always used it. So everyone becomes an aristocrat. Everyone can take holidays, but then you can get particular, as to whether you like holidays in the sun or are pleased with grey clouds, which I am. This, in a way, is establishing a new set of simultaneous equations, but they must be simultaneous, otherwise the money-unfairness comes out. Money just happens to be one of the items, but it can cancel out depending on the accuracy of the other parts of the equation. We've got to do that, you and I, and everyone working on it. I think that's enough, because a number of people would disagree with that, but only for a time, maybe. This distortion of time somehow leads to our discussion about museums. If you take Majorca, the entire island is a museum. People who enjoy that museum are enjoying things that they would never associate with conventional museums. But on holiday, they're enjoying the whole island as a museum. Therefore the "world museum" and the "world as a museum" are not far from each other. But we've got to work on that.

HUO – Is it a living museum?

CP – Yes, it's a living museum, but it should be unconsciously living. The living part of the museum is in fact as unconscious as the act of breathing, staying alive, so it impinges on all things, and therefore the nature of actually proposing such a museum must also encompass things that are as inevitable as daily breathing. It's no stranger than that. And who knows, holiday islands might be a good example, although the Walt Disney element is to be rejected in some way, to be played out. But not to be despised, that's the thing. In fact, you see, some criticisms, which I share, of theme parks are because they seem to be like Walt Disney, but they shouldn't be, or people feel they shouldn't be. It's a sort of moral code that perhaps theme parks and fun fairs are too serious to only be shared with Walt Disney. [...] If one makes the alternative museum almost into a birthright for everyone, then there's a danger that it will not be realized as being an additional, very valuable input to life. But I'm puzzled by what I've said, and you have an allergy, so we'll end this part, I think. It's a way of making exclusivity rather desirable without any snobbery at all. But I'm not quite sure about that. Maybe it's good to end on incompleteness.

The Conversation Series no 21: Cedric Price/Hans Ulrich Obrist
first published 2009, Verlag der Buchhandlung Walther König, Köln

SOCIAL EXCLUSION AND URBAN DESIGN

Ricky Burdett

The city of the future is facing major social challenges. Demographic change, the pluralization of cultures and lifestyles, and a growing social inequality manifested through spatial fragmentation are transforming urban society from the ground up — and in ways that often ignore a key ingredient for successful urban life: social inclusion.

This is of particular importance when one considers that half of the world's seven billion people live in an urban environment. By 2050, when the world's population is predicted to peak at nine billion, it's expected that 75 per cent of all humans will live in cities. Already today, cities such as Lagos, Delhi and Dhaka are growing by over 300,000 people a year. In addition to having a profound impact on the planet's ecological balance, the form that this new wave of urban construction takes will shape the human conditions for billions of people growing up and growing old in cities.

Cities by practical definition are magnets for diversity. They are natural areas of economic opportunity, which when properly fostered, result in social inclusion and mobility — two necessary factors in a healthy urban landscape and society at large. When functioning properly, the city is a machine of sorts that allows people to enrich their lot in life through improved access to education, health care, business, and networking. At their best, cities provide and nurture a civic space that encourages all of these desirable things to happen.

Unfortunately, the more one travels around the rapidly urbanizing regions of the world in Africa, in Asia, and in Latin America, the more one visits the centres and the outskirts of cities such as Johannesburg, Lima, New Delhi, or Dakar, you see examples of increasing exclusivity, with people of one type segregated from people of another. At one end, there is a growing landscape of gated communities for the wealthy, on the other social housing estates and slums for those at the bottom of the ladder. This is a pattern that is repeating itself across national and cultural boundaries.

Governments, public agencies, and the private sector are driving change to improve the living conditions of existing and new city dwellers. Unfortunately, in most instances this "change" is sadly outmoded. In Istanbul, for instance, the government is building three million housing units over twenty years, but the rows of bland, 20-storey towers surrounded by tarmac are reminiscent of the alienating social housing projects built across Europe and the United States in the mid-twentieth century. They may represent a basic human need — shelter — but they are dehumanizing. Rather than representing a promising trend in inclusivity, they are essentially an alienating ghettoization of less-fortunate populations.

As many Western cities are demolishing these impersonal and alienating housing developments owing to their social dysfunctionality, these projects are gaining in popularity in many developing nations. Similarly, as many Western nations have grown to increasingly rely on a combination of cultural preservation, increased urban density, and efficient public transportation, developing nations continue to draw on our past mistakes rather than time-tested improvements. As Mumbai attempts to redevelop Dharavi, India's largest slum, its efforts raise the spectre of the 1960s' "slum clearance" programmes that devastated the social life and urban structure of so many European and American cities. Similarly disheartening is São Paulo's continuous march towards endless sprawl, with four-hour commuting deemed acceptable in a city that accepts about one thousand new cars on its streets every day.

These sorts of projects represent a very different trajectory from Baron Haussmann's Paris or nineteenth-century London and New York, where people of very different backgrounds lived in relatively close proximity. Just as importantly, the different functions of everyday life — sleeping, going to school, shopping, or going to work — tended to be relatively close to each other. Greater proximity and greater density lead to exactly what cities are good at — mixing together people of different backgrounds. Dense, well-connected, and well-designed cities not only make good social sense; they also make good economic and environmental sense, as they are far more sustainable than sprawl. Suburbia leads to a disaggregation and a fragmentation of city life, which promotes exclusion, poor assimilation, and environmental waste through inherently poor public transportation across unnecessarily scattered destinations (hospitals, housing, schools, shopping, work, etc).

While there is no perfect, one-size fits all remedy to promote integration and inclusivity, owing to obvious cultural and demographic differences among the world's cities, from an urban design and planning point of view, the well-connected "open city" — where life is lived "on the street" — is a very powerful design tool. If you look at the cities that feel open, accessible, and integrated, it will be because of some combination of these design ingredients, as well as a strong emphasis on public transportation.

Consider the streets of Barcelona, New York, or London: they are not especially similar to one another, but they do share certain key characteristics, such as pedestrian access and public and business uses at the ground level, i.e. retail shops, offices, and public promenades. One is able to walk freely from one urban use to another without having to cross boundaries or gates. These are the makings of an open and potentially democratic city. It is the encouragement of day-to-day social and transactional encounters between diverse groups of people that keeps society going. This is where an inclusive design of the city comes into play. The public spaces of cities, the squares, the parks, the alleyways, and the streets themselves become the social glue that keeps society together.

Similarly, an open, inclusive city must have a reliable, affordable, and extensive public transportation network. It is precisely in the sorts of cities that are growing so rapidly in developing nations that people must have an open transport system to get to work, and by doing so better their family's economic future. Public transportation is a critical element allowing everyone to partake in all the advantages urban life has to offer. And it doesn't have to be luxurious — Bogotá's TransMilenio is a simple system incorporating buses, but it's well designed and very effective for moving people around a city of seven million.

Ultimately, cities can both brutalize and humanize people and the environment. Which way they go depends on governance and leadership. If you think of the success of Barcelona or Copenhagen or Rome, it's because for hundreds of years there has always been purposeful investment in their public spaces. City leaders have an opportunity to make a difference, building on the spatial and social DNA of their cities, rather than importing generic models that cater to the homogenizing forces of globalization. A well-run and designed city represents the nexus of good planning, architecture and local politics. It takes cooperation amongst these disciplines to make real and fairly rapid change. Change at the local level, if inspired and persistent, is as significant as good urban leadership and a strong metropolitan vision. The rediscovering of the fragile thread that links physical order to human behaviour will be the main task of enlightened leadership in a world where, for better or worse, 75 per cent of us will soon be living in urban environments.

SPACES FOR INTERPRETATION
R.B. Parkinson

The migration of ancient artefacts can be an excitingly ambivalent process. In the case of the famous Rosetta Stone, it is what creates its modem meaning. Around 196 BCE, this inscription was erected at the Egyptian temple of Sais; in the medieval period it was moved as a building block to el-Rashid (Rosetta), and was then discovered by Napoleon's troops in 1799 and brought to Europe. In antiquity, it was simply a standard copy of a decree that was set up in every temple in the land, but its transport transformed it into the key to the European decipherment of Ancient Egyptian hieroglyphs. Its subsequent life-story as an icon of decipherment has reached extraordinary distances, with its name being given to a European Space Agency probe that 'deciphers' the composition of comets.

Such movements can also pose risks. In the 1820s the British consul-general in Egypt, Henry Salt, acquired some wall-paintings with 'scenes of daily life' from the tomb-chapel of an ancient official at Luxor, the accountant Nebamun, buried around 1350 BCE. Salt's local agent removed these from the walls of the chapel, destroying much of it as he did so, and shipped them to England. Without such action, these wall-paintings might not have survived, and since then they have been almost continually on public display in the British Museum, giving these masterly works an audience that their painters could not have foreseen. But such accessibility was at the price of a bewildering loss of context, and in their early twentieth century displays they seemed so abstracted from their original space that art historians occasionally described them as 'panel paintings'. Originally they decorated the walls of a brilliantly painted tiny chamber, less than 2 metres high and only some 1.5 metres wide. Such a space is impossible to recreate literally within a museum gallery that must accommodate over five million visitors a year. But without a feeling of this space, their impact on the viewer is fragmented and diminished. In the course of conservation work and analysis, it became apparent that the most virtuosic and entertaining areas of painting — a group of musicians looking out at the viewer, a flock of geese in a flurry of white, grey, and black feathers — were placed exactly at the viewer's eye level. And all was executed to be seen in the soft half-light of the chapel by family members and passers-by, commemorating the dead. The paintings were intended for the human eye, with memory, affection and face to face intimacy.

In grand neo-classical museum rooms such feelings can easily be lost, and so for the new display in 2009, a hanging ceiling was placed in the gallery to make it seem more intimate. The fragments were re-mounted so that they could be viewed as parts of a single wall of colour, and the display space was surrounded by limestone panels evoking the colour and texture of the original landscape. Low light levels (necessary for conservation) helped to establish a still, calm and meditative atmosphere, recreating the effect that we believe the original chamber will have had on the ancient viewers. This evocation of a lost ancient space is, in one sense, simply a practical issue of design and display, but it is also at the intellectual heart of interpretation, to enable modern viewers to continue the processes of interpretation begun by their ancient predecessors.

Even with Ancient Egyptian poetry, which might be considered a contextually free, autonomous art-form, modern spaces have a transformative effect on interpretation. The best known surviving poem, *The Tale of Sinuhe* from 1850 BCE, can seem on the academic printed page to be a somewhat propagandistic narrative of an official life, but when it is moved into a more performative face to face context, closer to the manner in which it was originally experienced, it becomes a rapid, passionate and questioning experience. Most surprisingly, the text's meanings are revealed to be remarkably unstable and open: in one recital in the Museum's great Egyptian sculpture gallery, the poem's praises of the pharaoh rang out with moderate conviction, amid the poet's subtle qualifications. But in a smaller more intimate auditorium at the Ledbury Poetry festival, arguably more evocative of the original performance spaces, these praises sounded suddenly ironic and hollow, even though the poem was recited by the same actors, in the same translation and with the same emphases. A movement into new environments can open up the meanings of a familiar text or artefact, reminding us of the contingency of all interpretation, and reshaping the ways in which viewers engage with these ancient works. We can never fully recover the original contexts of ancient art, but by evoking them by what means we have, we can help establish a continuity of reception and open up possibilities of fresh engagements by modern audiences. The trick is to find a space — intellectual, physical and/ or social — that will enable and sustain these possibilities.

24 APRIL CONVERSATION
Oscar Niemeyer & Paulo Sergio Niemeyer

Oscar Niemeyer:

'What surprises me when I look through my work as an architect is to verify that in the last ten years – the last five years, to be precise – I have worked harder than in my entire life. It is on these latter projects, more complex than the previous ones, that I would like to express myself. I must comment only on the Pampulha complex - my first job as an architect.

What amazes me is to feel that at that time (sixty years ago) my thoughts on architecture were exactly the same as the ones I advocate today. The search for a different form that would generate surprise, the desire for concrete in all its possibilities, and the concern for integration between the arts and architecture were already part of my ideas as an architect. And all this explains the Pampulha Church, covered in curves, the large panel of *azulejos* [ceramic tiles] that, at my request, were prepared by Portinari, the low reliefs by Ceschiatti and Paulo Werneck's drawings. And the Pampulha Church, was commented on around the whole world, at that time when all religious architecture suffered prejudice.'

Paulo Sergio Niemeyer:

Paulo Sergio Niemeyer, architect, urban planner and designer, committed in achieving a result and a visual communication style capable of arousing global concern, follows strictly the influence of his great-grandfather, Oscar Niemeyer, in his works.

He understands the attributes of lightness and sinuosity which identify the works of Oscar Niemeyer, and seeks to meet the contemporary demands of sustainability.

"My work embraces values nurtured for decades by my great-grandfather, Oscar Niemeyer. This influence on my upbringing has led me to partake in this ceaseless struggle for a more sympathetic and fraternal world, where beauty has its central place."

LEARNING AND WORKING AROUND THE WORLD
Álvaro Siza Vieira

Text when entering the Acropolis

San Francisco Church in Goa

Plan for Macau

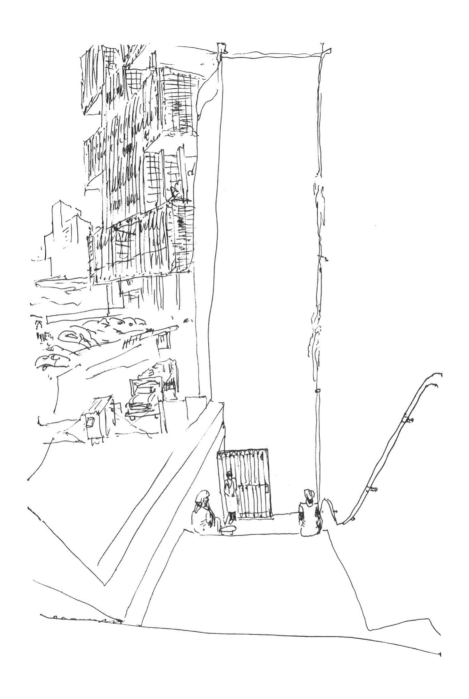

Old and New in Rio de Janeiro

THOUGHTS ON ARCHITECTURE AND PLANNING
Aaron Betsky

The first fact that we must confront in architecture and design is that we do not need more things. We have enough chairs, buildings and cities. We do not need to waste more natural resources on making structures. This is especially true in the realm of architecture, where almost all new construction will be of worse quality than what it replaces and whatever we build will have to be adapted or changed almost as soon as it is finished. This is due to the fact that we invest less and less in our real world. Value engineering is the symptom of the larger attempt to make capital move as quickly as possible. Not only money moves at ever increasing rates, so do people and goods. We live in the just-in-time, flextime world, in which fixed structures are a hindrance.

For these reasons, we do not need new buildings. We need better interiors; places that will make us feel at home in our modern world. We need to enscene our lives so that we can play the roles we see as fitting with those we want to be our fellow actors. Architecture should be a tool that allows us to do so. It should be scaffolding, scene building, and sequencing. It should also be built as quickly and cheaply as possible.
This is also true because of course we can no longer afford to use up scarce natural resources. All buildings should not only be net producers of energy, they should also not use any new natural resources.

At the smaller scale, the last thing we need is more chairs, tables, lamps, or other furniture. We need to make what we have smart, and make it more comfortable. We should recombine and rethink what we have.

At the larger scale, we must confront a world of sprawl. That means not just the growth of exurbs and suburbs, but the thinning of the inner city as well. It also means the stretching of individual spaces, as the requirements each person has for his or her own domain continue to grow. Space is the ultimate luxury, and it produces sprawl. Sprawl also causes its own counter-movement, towards increasing densification in pockets. Though some see this as positive, I would point out that the piling up of people and goods, even if they are around public transit stops, is not altogether pleasant. It also creates huge waste in terms of getting things, people, and data in and out. The relationship between thin and dense is also one of increasing social and economic stratification.

Sprawl itself is no more than a symptom of the disappearance of all fixed social and economic, and thus political, relations. The state falls apart, as does the corporation, the family, and every other bond that used to tie us together. Even the body falls apart and is infested with technology. Design cannot pretend to be a bulwark against these movements. It will only wind up either exacerbating them if it does, or failing.

Moreover, in this sprawling world of continual change and movement, planning that presumes the carrying out of fixed structures according to a prearranged scheme makes less and less sense. Without dictatorial bureaucracies, whether governmental or private, we cannot tell people where to live, work or play. We can only provide incentives and project scenarios. These need to be as flexible as possible.

Buildings have become monuments, which is to say memorials to past ways of living and thinking. They have become the tomb of architecture. Urban planning has become a way to sell real estate or vouchsafe power. It has become the burial ground of urban life. What we need is to design ourselves out of the future and towards the present by rethinking, remaking, reusing, and opening up what we have inherited.

Winnipeg

White sheet of paper
Hildegard Weber

We have efficient analytical ways of facilitating the search — a plume of chemicals in a river,
even a missing child, a plan B in which sun rays are reflected back into space
to stop climate change.
Mother Nature demonstrates compelling solutions. A simulation of how some white blood cells seek to
destroy infectious particles, shows how life forms — like cells, sharks or bees —
successfully find a target, with limited information and even more limited cognitive skills.
But don't we want to escape the slavery of the analytical and just follow our guts?
Life can be so much more enjoyable. Let the pigeons fly, the mice crawl —
birds are highly skilled at planning travel routes,
an ability we are chasing. As we rely so much on transportation and shipping, we try to control them
to perfection. As we humans are not having enough resources and capacities,
we are bound to leave this job to Computers.
At Cern, a broken cable has almost turned relativity theory upside down.

Zeitgeist = process = migration

I did it, you did it too. We all grabbed a pen and drew Euler's House of Santa Claus.
Connecting 8 straight lines without retracing one of them, sometimes more, sometimes less successfully.
Euler's circuits set milestones in fields like graph theory, ecology, sociology. Needless to say, they are
also applicable to genome sequencing, parametric design process, music arrangements including
the hunt for planets and the apparently efficient chase of potential criminal suspects.
In such instances a systematic and reassuring search is essential to make all information available.
Organisms, on the other hand, do that already; they use strategies like chemotaxis, or an already-known
search pattern, or a combination of both, that work better in their existing non-ideal environments.
So, who is that man in the house of Santa Claus?
He is jet setting around the world 24/7, benefitting from earth being a ball of total freedom,
of 360 degrees unhindered view. Were the Pyramids built for him, the natives waiting for him?
Shopping in New York, in airplanes, buses, trains — can he locate himself between the alien and the
self-evident? One thing is for sure, Motels always have a clean pillow.
Does this make him a perfect patient of Sigmund Freud?
What newspapers did on a regional scale was the initial purpose of the Internet and TV news globally:
sharing unopiniated and trusted knowledge and news. But then came Facebook, Wiki and Twitter. The digital
revolution has changed the mentality and appreciation.
Bucky Fuller was one of the global and holistic thinkers. He explored synergies of principles of energy and
material efficiency. But being a critical mind,
he saw previous utopian schemes as too exclusive, and thought that was
a major source of their failure. In 1970 he wrote, "I live on Earth at present, and
I don't know where I am. I know that I am not a category. I am not a thing - a noun.
I seem to be a verb, an evolutionary process — an integral function of the Universe".
The dream of the Ideal starts with a master plan, either in an urban, political, or economic sense:
designed with uniforming criteria. The ideal is intriguing and absolutely necessary.
The current "occupy" movement is an example. We have the liberty to be free, better,
we have the duty. But I want to know: does endless freedom bore Santa Claus or is he happy to be back in the
house with cross bars like a prison — or is my home my castle? Sometimes I explore ugly, dilapidated houses with
brick walls, doors, and windows that can occasionally be seen between impersonal pieces of high-tech palaces —
their "No" to houses, doors and windows is challenged
by graffiti on some walls between them. It is a contradiction, and lures one to stop.
They may be ugly and disturbing. It shows high-risk behaviour in public space
and reminds us of what is needed to get involved.
The city is the spatial forum of community; don't forget the beggars, squatters, children, elderly...
the creative in all nations. Are architectural and social forms not characterized
by their density and proximity?
The silent relicts of abandoned buildings - they scream or whisper. Bricked out windows and doors
make the Taboo even more obvious.
I try to peel off layers - reveal history and tales, take away their defence mechanism - photographically
and with movies. Responsible citizens want to participate, take to the streets,
demonstrating their honest resentments. They also know how to distinguish advertising from art, they
know what it is, they have a voice and choice. Art is a sign of individual action, it's needed; that works both
positively and negatively. We are disorder in order — it is time to oppose exactly what the people love to think
about art! Enlightened questioning, defoliating the Why, is no longer a taboo. Disenchantment should have
no place here. Retain both "taboo" and not "taboo" - undo inviolability. We can influence the emotions, the
human condition — we are not alone.
"Art is the daughter of liberty" (Schiller) — they both have to stay indefinite, young and fresh.
I take an eraser to remove the lines of Euler's house, set the man free, hand him back over to intuition.
A white sheet of paper again...

Palisades Glacier

River

Bedburg Hau

Venice

Berlin

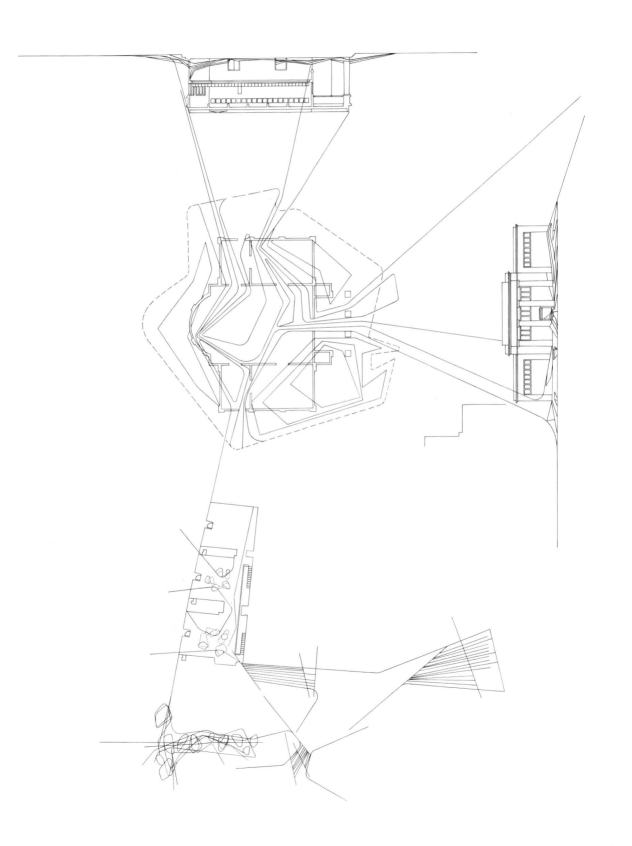

SHIFTING GROUND
Beatrice Galilee

I should preface this brief essay on the increasing irrelevance of building in architecture by saying I have a favourite building. A tiny chapel in a field in northern Germany so quiet and whole with poetry and humanity, it is humbling to be in its presence.

The Bruder Klaus chapel was designed by Peter Zumthor. The imprints of its seven-year-long construction, the layers of materials and methods used to create a tiny cradle-like space are tangible to all senses. The chapel, built in 2007, stands for a timeless architecture rooted in philosophy and phenomenology.

For all its inestimable quality, this is an architecture that is fundamentally at odds with the reality - or migration - of practice today. To situate it in contemporary language, Zumthor's aleatoric craft belongs to the one per cent.

And what of the 99 per cent? Informal architecture practice makes up the world's cities, sprawling mountains of homes, lives, constructions. But increasingly the tactics and techniques used to practise architecture from the bottom up are finding themselves more relevant.

The procurement processes and financial systems that rooted western architectural production into a "single client-single architect" model have faltered. With depression-crisis-austerity cycles seeing no end in Europe, unemployment for the next generation of architects is inevitable. Instead of going underground, young architects are entering into collaborative, investigative, political modes of architectural, technological and spatial practice.

The so-called "Third Industrial Revolution"[1] of crowd-sourced funding, open source design and advanced fabrication has transformed the notion of a bottom-up approach from idealistic, niche practice into a valid and well-used strategy for self-funding projects. Some of these projects, the Wikihouse and Open Architecture Network to name two, deal with real-world building problems using open-sourced, creative-commons licensed designs. The WikiHouse produces not just construction details, but construction-ready parts. Like an IKEA-house of one's own design. But it is not necessarily the built elements of this work that count.

Studios and collaborative teams see architectural practice as something much more expansive, more open to question. Far more interesting than finding a client, a site and a budget, is pro-actively solving or producing spatial conditions.

This practice has had its moments in the spotlight. In the sixties and seventies, SuperStudio were railing at architects to be more political and to defy any architecture that was an affirmation of the "bourgeois model of ownership and society". The role of an architect as a social-practitioner has been suppressed by the recent role of the architect as a king-maker, a producer of culture and a regenerator of cities.

In conditions where the state refuses to invest in culture and increasingly washes its hands of social problems, then spatial practice in terms of political lobbying, campaigning, occupying can take on those responsibilities. The overtly public nature of the Occupy Movement and the Arab Spring demonstrate that collectivity is not just about protest, but about demanding - and sometimes winning - political change.

We must also acknowledge that architectural engagement practice now happens through new formats that bear no relationship to bricks and mortar, and that the spatial practitioner needs to find new strategies to come closer to this new public, audience, or client. Architects, sociologists, urban planners, social activists confront civic issues by helping to build the common social spaces of their cities from the bottom up. They interact with politicians, policy-makers and community groups, and participate collaboratively in the construction of more equitable sustainable cities.

The notion of architect as civic entrepreneur is perhaps less important than the migration in the concept of civic entrepreneur as architect.

[1] "The Third Industrial Revolution", *The Economist*, 21 April, 2011

STRATIGRAPHIES OF MIND
Michael Jansen

A hot, humid day in January 1982; the lush green of the palm trees stands in sharp contrast to the white of the churches; Old Goa, the former seat of the viceroy of the Portuguese colonial empire. We were on a short holiday from the dry, dusty excavations in Mohenjo-Daro close to the mighty river Indus, close to Larkana, the home town of Zulfikar Ali Bhutto who was hanged in 1979 by the new ruler of Pakistan, General Zia ul Haq. Every year, during our winter campaign in Mohenjo-Daro, the largest bronze-age city in the world, we escaped from the extremely hard conditions in the middle of nowhere to the green paradise that is Goa - a few days holiday, fresh fish in one of the shacks close to the beach, a Kingfisher beer, in the night swimming naked in the warm Indian Ocean under a big round yellow moon. Sometimes our bodies were like neon lights in the water: the plankton made them visible. We were full of joy.

Mohenjo-Daro, cold nights in dark green tents, charpoys literally "four legs", wooden frames with a filling made of cord strings, the mattress made of cotton, hidden in sleeping bags, our few belongings scattered on the reed mats that covered the ground. A steel table with books and drawing equipment. Electricity for naked bulbs from a generator sponsored by Siemens Pakistan. Four months away from home, from entertainment, from a good beer. We get up at seven, breakfast, work on site: documentation on 40 kilometres of excavated brick walls, 4,500 years old, re-checking of 100,000 square metres of former excavations. K.N. Dikshit 1922, Vats 1925, R.D. Banerji 1924, Harold Hargreaves 1926, Ernest Mackay 1927, later, in 1945 and 1950 the famous archaeologist and British brigadier who fought in Africa against Rommel, Sir Mortimer Wheeler. The last large-scale excavation was in 1965 by the American archaeologist George Dales. Then we came, checked what had been done to newly interpret what had been said before. We also looked for new evidence on the unexcavated surface. Together with our Italian colleagues, we used for the first time an unmanned hot air balloon "Aachen" to carefully record the archaeological surface and found wonderful new things. The nights were cold, sometimes coming down to freezing point. It was dark by six. The night watchmen came, made fires, sometimes played their flutes. We joined them after dinner. Now and then the silence of the night was broken by the cries of a hyena. The evenings were long before we could sleep: no television, sometimes radio. The first four weeks were the worst. In the evening we were nervous, wanted to do something, some entertainment, running away from the need to feel the time. Later we got used to the new feeling of time, and sat with the watchmen at the fire for hours, doing nothing, looking into the Glut???, listening to the flute. The Indus Civilization in the third millennium BC was one of the three early civilizations of the world. Civilizations have, *per definitionem*, writing. What is writing and why was it invented? Definitely it had to do with the developed complexity of cultures, which expanded so much that the socio-political religious? systems had to develop something like a recording and communication system to be stored and also communicated. The first writing in Mesopotamia was for registration within the temple economy, not poem or literature, not religious texts. Unfortunately the writing of the Indus Civilization has not yet been deciphered. Bad luck for us, as we do not yet know how this civilization functioned. We know more or less about Ancient Egypt and Mesopotamia. Writing always was and remains today an important means to transfer knowledge. How long this will remain, we do not know.

The only church in Old Goa that is not whitewashed is Bom Jesus built in 1592, more than 15,000 km by sea from Europe. This was not long after Vignola's Il Gesù in Rome, supposed to be the first Baroque architecture. Both were built for the new Jesuit order founded by Ignatius of Loyola as a tool against the new Protestant church. The IHS sign (one of the readings is: *Iesus Hominum Salvator*) became the Jesuit token of the Catholic Counter Reformation after the Council of Trent (*Concilium Tridentinum*) in 1545-1563. This IHS can be seen prominently at the top of Bom Jesus, the church in which the friend and co-founder of the Jesuits, Francis Xavier is buried. To show the "glory of God on earth" was one of their strategies. The overwhelming gold with which the altar fronts in the Goan churches are covered even today impresses visitors.

How did this baroque church building come to Portuguese Goa, thousands of kilometres from Rome and Christian Europe? Looking at it, I started speculating: the time span of the completion of Il Gesù in Rome (1568-75) and Bom Jesus (1595-1605) in Goa was hardly thirty years or the time span of one generation. In those days a trip by ship from Europe to India took several months, not to mention the dangers of sailing along the coasts around Africa and the Cape of Good Hope. But who travelled? If famous architects had built this church, their name would have been known. Doubtless the layout of the inner church was designed according to Jesuit rules: an open space dominated by the high altar and the pulpit for sermons: everybody inside the church could see the priest preaching from the pulpit. But outside, the fascinating detailed façade with the IHS in a large circle in the gable was unique. Even if the figures indicated the influence of local craftsmen, the brilliance of the composition must have had European minds behind it. And for whom was this church built? For the local Indian Christians? For the Indian pagans to demonstrate the power of the Catholic church?

Looking at the façade I had another idea. During the sixteenth century, the fast dissemination of information had just started through the application of the new technique of printing books with movable letters, invented by Gutenberg around 1440 in Mainz, Germany. Would it have been feasible that this new style of European architecture came to Goa through printed knowledge? Renaissance architecture especially in its Mannerist??? forms had been strongly influenced by another, newly discovered written record, almost 1,500 years old, Vitruvius's *Ten Books on Architecture*. Alberti had been dealing with them and Serlio's version was printed and widely distributed using the new printing techniques around 1540, just a few decades before Bom Jesus was built. Shortly after Serlio's publication the boom started and printed catalogues of architectural orders and instructions on how to build churches, forts, palaces were disseminated all over the world. The new architectural 'style' was fast adopted from North and South America to South-East Asia, leaving the first global imprints of a 'global' formal architectural language. It goes without saying that in the course of European colonisation not only its forms, but also its values spread wherever colonialism took place. With the invention of the printed book as a written source and its easy distribution all over the world, the travelling of *homo creativus (faber)* had been widely substituted by the travelling of instruction books.

2008: We are making a film with Arte on Pakistan, the river Indus and Mohenjo-Daro. From Islamabad we leave in March for the first shooting in the Karakorum. Owing to bad weather we cannot fly to Gilgit but have to take the Karakorum Highway, which is muddy and dangerous. Halfway we get stuck. The road has been blocked by an avalanche; hundreds of cubic metres of snow and ice have come down and are blocking the road. The Indus river flows thunderously 50 metres below. After many hours the army has cleared the road with heavy machinery. We are in the Hunza valley. I sit in our small hotel; wifi is available. I get a phone call from Aachen. It is my secretary asking normal things. Thirty years ago in Mohenjo-Daro it took me almost a day to make a phone call to Germany: travel to Larkana, 35 kilometres away, go to the post office, register the call, wait for endless time. The call comes, booked for three minutes because of the cost. Then the emptiness when the call is over.

The age of books, of travelling knowledge by printed matter is soon over! Now we have the Internet, we have mobile phones; I wrote my last letter to my beloved a long time ago, with the shortage of time and efficacy of communication today, I simply phone. How exciting it used to be in the camp in Mohenjo-Daro when the postman came. He rode an old bicycle, a man with a long white beard, no post man's uniform, with the firewood he had collected on his back rack. I always thought that he was the "man from the moon". The letters were wonderful: homesickness, love, information on what had happened 8,000 kilometres away. I sit in Skardu and exchange more or less important news with the word???, answering mail. Tomorrow we will begin filming: a Polo game and I am the honoured guest.

Why can't we be in different places at the same time? Till now the time-space law (whatever that is) prohibits it. The first time I saw the giant buddhas of Bamiyan I came from Europe by local bus, travelling overland to India. I was 23 and looking for the fulfilment of a desire to move in time and space. The strange, the unknown made me move.

In 2002 I stayed a second time in front of them, the niches were like the eyes of a blind man. I was 55 and still looking for the fulfilment of a desire to move in time and space. The same place, another time, empty niches, buddhas broken into pieces, lying on the bottom of the niches. 1500 years, same place, same niches, monks around, adoration, songs, peace. Imagination, *genius loci*.

Ancient writing in Mohenjo-Daro, mass printing in the sixteenth century, surfing through the Internet today. Where is the improvement? In relation to what?

While I am completing this text I am sitting in my room in the Serena hotel in Kabul; today is the first day of May, 2012. We are working on "culture for peace" in Afghanistan. In 2013 the city of Ghazni will be "Cultural Capital of Islam"; in 2014 the ISAF troops will be moving out. Yesterday we had a meeting: Mes Aynak, a newly discovered, fantastic site of the Gandhara Culture dating from the 4th-5th century AD will be destroyed by a Chinese mining company. The site is on a copper mine. The World Bank will be financing the emergency rescue.

Carpo, Mario, *Architecture in the Age of Printing: Orality, Writing, Typography, and printed images in the history of architectural history*, MIT, 2001
Leon Battista Alberti, *De re aedificatoria*, 1443-1452

AFTER PHYSICS
Victoria Bell

In New Mexico space & time are odd,
because a road sign or other recognizable
object distant in time & space partly hidden
by a hill in the landscape will look in the
strong light & colour just as sharp as if it were
a few feet away and immediate. The mountains
far away look much closer, and you can't tell
how big they are because they are fractal,
self-scaling. So you can play around with
the space between, and everything is accessible,
with no layers of atmosphere or weather
between, in the magical space & time, just like
in outer space where the stars seem
accessible just using gravity to reach them.

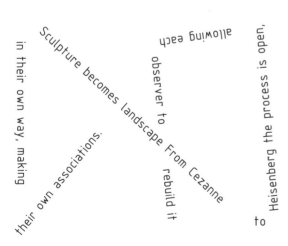

Sculpture becomes landscape From Cezanne to Heisenberg the process is open, allowing each observer to rebuild it in their own way, making their own associations.

ENERGY BACK TO THE SUN

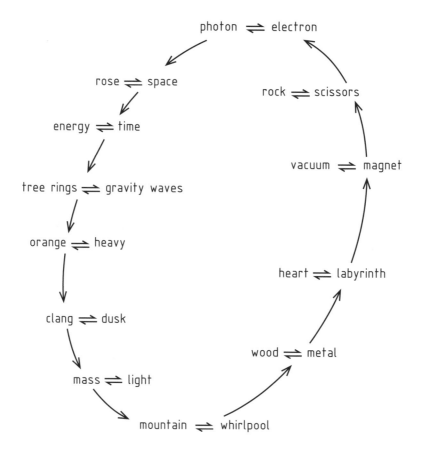

photon ⇌ electron

rose ⇌ space

energy ⇌ time

tree rings ⇌ gravity waves

orange ⇌ heavy

clang ⇌ dusk

mass ⇌ light

mountain ⇌ whirlpool

wood ⇌ metal

heart ⇌ labyrinth

vacuum ⇌ magnet

rock ⇌ scissors

SPACETIME GETS FATTER

of my sculptures are in a place where they don't

I have dreams now where parts

these parts are from

sculptures I haven't made yet.

The meaning is

belong or strangers have colonized

the use.

parts of my studio. On waking I realize

In modern physics (after Lee Smolin & others)
you can build up spacetime starting with
events, not atoms as the basic unit. Imagine a
network of interlocking changes, both like & unlike,
from the tiny transitions between electrons &
photons, to tree growth & weather, unfolding
with or without your "walking" them, to gravitational
waves changing neighbouring stars.
Pressure on earth increases the flow from
one locus to another in the network, making space
travel more & more likely. With the memory of
earth's diversity on the retina, one travels on
G-waves to barren worlds, initiating the
evolution of new species half invented (midway
between one era & the next) & half stimulated
by the new environment.

Cologne

Dubai

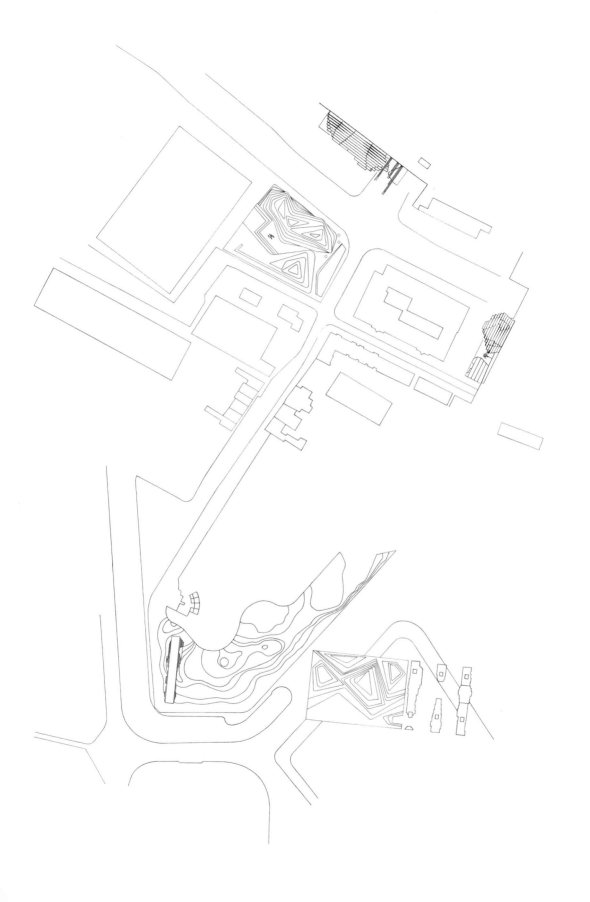

MIGRATION OF A VIRUS
Marcus Altfeld

Human migration and loss of social roots represent one of the important risk factors for the spread of the Human Immunodeficiency Virus (HIV). Migration and adaptation of HIV within/to a newly infected host is a race against space and time, which the virus unfortunately wins in most cases. However, these sometimes subtle adaptations ("murmuring") of the virus also allow us scientists to identify the Achilles heel of the virus and to hopefully develop a protective vaccine.

HIV is a master in exploiting its evolutionary space, hiding in the very same immune cells that should fight the virus, and rapidly adapting to the infected host. This allows HIV to evade the human immune defences and to survive for many years, eventually killing the infected person in the absence of therapy. During those years, the virus has plenty of opportunities to be transmitted to new individuals, taking advantage of one of our fundamental human needs, sexual contact. UNAIDS estimated that 34 million individuals were living with HIV at the end of 2010, most of them in Sub-Saharan Africa, and that approximately 1.8 million individuals died of AIDS in 2010 alone. Furthermore, there were 2.7 million new HIV infections in 2010, including an estimated 390,000 among children.

How does it come about that this virus is so successful in spreading through the human population, and so difficult to control? HIV permanently integrates itself into the DNA of a newly infected person within days, making elimination of the virus almost impossible. Following an initial localized infection at the site of infection, HIV migrates to almost all compartments of the human body, creating a systemic infection. Every day, more than a billion new viruses are produced in an infected individual, and each of these viruses can be slightly different from the other ones, creating a tremendous viral diversity. Most importantly, any attempts by the immune system to fight HIV are neutralized by rapid evolution of the virus, changing in areas the immune system tries to recognize, and thereby remaining largely invisible. Being a master of disguise, and overwhelming through sheer numbers and diversity, HIV eventually exhausts the defence systems of an infected person.

However, despite the ability of HIV-1 to rapidly change in order to evade any attempts at control, there are limits within the space in which the virus can evolve. HIV has to remain HIV, and cannot change indefinitely – and this is the one Achilles heel that has allowed scientists to gain some ground against the epidemic. In the mid-1990s, physicians realized that while HIV was able to easily evade control attempted by the use of a single antiviral drug, the use of at least three different drugs at the same time was successful in suppressing HIV replication. Attacking HIV simultaneously on three different fronts overwhelmed the ability of the virus to escape, restricted the evolutionary space by cornering the virus, and resulted in a dramatic decrease in morbidity and mortality in those HIV-infected individuals that have access to life-saving therapy. Unfortunately, the majority of HIV-infected individuals live in parts of the world in which the health systems are not able to provide treatment for everyone, and still two new people are infected for any person starting treatment. Furthermore, the current treatments cannot cure the infection, and require life-long use of medication. Nevertheless, the introduction of antiviral treatment has been an important milestone in our journey to reduce the suffering and death caused by HIV.

The most successful approach to end the HIV epidemic will be the development of a vaccine that prevents infection. Attempts to develop such a vaccine over the past two-three decades have been unsuccessful. The tremendous diversity of the virus and its ability to rapidly adapt to any immune pressure constitute huge barriers for a protective vaccine. However, there have been several recent successes that provide hope. Instead of just fearing the ability of the virus to rapidly evolve and escape any external attempts to restrict its replication, the evolutionary space within which the viruses migrates, and the trajectories the virus chooses might hold the answers to a successful attack, demarcating the vulnerable regions within HIV. Very detailed investigations of these escape pathways used by HIV have now allowed scientists to define the routes that the viruses can take to evade the immune system, but also the dead ends and barriers the virus cannot cross. Parts of the virus simply do not allow for any significant changes without disrupting its architecture and function. The attempts of HIV to protect those areas have therefore now started to help scientists to develop vaccines that target specifically those Achilles heels of the virus. The hope is that targeting multiple vulnerable spots within the virus at the same time with a vaccine will compromise the ability of HIV to escape, like the successful approach used by antiviral drugs.

Given the global dimension of the HIV epidemic, affecting every continent of the world, and significant differences between HIV strains that circulate in different parts of the world, the development of a global HIV vaccine has to be a collaborative effort, involving communities and scientists worldwide. While human migration, in particular migration resulting from economic needs, such as migrant workers, represents a significant risk factor for HIV infection, the answer to this devastating epidemic will also be facilitated through migration and communication – getting bright and dedicated people together to collaboratively and collectively decipher the architecture of this virus, to identify its weak points and target them, and thus put an end to HIV and AIDS.

LAYERS OF FACT AND FICTION – MAPPING
Rita Kersting

Imaginative and imaginary architecture by He.Lo architects.

The stability of architecture, its quality as fixed structure, in general immobile and long-lasting, expressing the ideological and technical possibilities of specific times and places is fundamentally questioned in the work of He.Lo architects. Sónia Nunes Henriques' and Jan-Maurits Loecke's thinking about architecture starts with material, which has nothing to do with 'material material' like stone, wood, steel, concrete or glass but rather contextual features such as sound and stillness, sunlight and shadows, and a high awareness of architecture as bridging and connecting structure inform their experimental approach. Their design proposals for specific architectural projects such as the new Mosque in Cologne, the German Pavilion in Venice, a City Crossing in Winnipeg or urban regeneration in New York reveal He.Lo's unbiased and caring contextual approach.

'Mapping' is not a proposal for a building, a main crossing, or a new quarter; it is not a detailed model to be executed on a larger scale; it is an abstract manifesto, a retrospective resumé of He.Lo's oeuvre so far in the form of imaginary maps. And it is a composition that can be interpreted – like notation for music, graphics for sociology or a work of art initiating communication.

In 'Mapping', a series of nine drawings (each 594 x 420 cm), the interconnected quality of architecture, as well as its possibility to integrate and transform into landscape and history is presented two-dimensionally. The form of a map is used in an intriguing way: 'Mapping' means mirroring the real, classically gaining power through exact knowledge of the landscape – documented, defined, and depicted from a bird's-eye perspective. He.Lo's mappings, however, are inventions based on the idea of the fluidity of formerly stable truths combining factual architectural, geological and landscape elements with fictitious features. The written names of the cities offer a hint to the different projects, but in stitching together the drawings of the various places, they move far beyond: they create new neighbourhoods, immediate vicinities of faraway cities and cultures. In this sense, 'Mapping' links the motives of history and the future, of once upon a time and utopia. The abstract depictions serve to apprehend the (im-)possible simultaneity of Ho Chi Minh City? and Valence, of Cologne and Glacier Palisades. Or of Ceuta and Bonn, two small places that recall the political impact that a city name can have. The former German capital symbolises a time capsule after the Second World War: Western alliance, prospering consumerism, a place of democracy and protest; Ceuta in Spain is a place of existential hope and despair, the most African place in Europe, connecting and disrupting the two continents. Linking these two cities, for example by drawing lines representing geological or architectural structures, leads to a nearly surreal confrontation. Lautréamont wrote that beauty was the chance meeting of a sewing-machine and an umbrella on a dissecting-table.

On the other hand, *'Mapping'* also shows an approach that is characterized by authenticity. Reading carefully the surrounding and interlocking urban events it pays respect to the spatial and cultural heritage of each place, challenging generalizing globalization. He.Lo's architecture is a modern site archaeology and is of a highly analytical nature. It is about peeling off the layers of history while creating identity and intimacy of space. He.Lo's structures emerge mostly from geographic and urban topography, but with their specific use of straight lines they draw a line between the organic and the orthogonal man-made. No space is neglected, backstage doesn't exist. They accentuate the sites not only as a repository of meaning, but call attention to the edge of the space and its relationship to the site beyond.

Next to their continuous interdisciplinary research, He.Lo's work is characterized by the way they listen to the surroundings and urban events. The unintentional plays an important role in their design and adds an aspect that can be qualified as human. The architects' work opens a dialogue with the arts and music, especially with New Music by Cage, Stockhausen, Kagel. Cage's fundamental musical turn which integrates unintentional sound as well as the freedom to compose while interpreting, is an influential source. Also his special way of notation finds an echo in the incredibly fine, analogue hand drawings by the architects. He.Lo's affiliation to music illustrates for example the invitation of Wilhelm Bruck. He uses instruments as a landscape for fingers and adds a new dimension to the imagined rivers, hills, mountains and seas merging with the featured parametric, topographic, dynamic or permeable structures and bridges around the world.

In the age of digital visualization *'Mapping'* follows the tradition of early architectural and scientific hand-drawing, a playful innuendo to Piranesi's fantastic chalk drawings, Alexander von Humboldt's botanical studies, or the detailed drawings by Enric Miralles, with whom Nunes Henriques and Loecke worked in Barcelona.

As authors of *Spatial Murmuring* Jan-Maurits Loecke and Sonia Nunes Henriques brought together protagonists of different disciplines: artists, scientists, archaeologists, philosophers, sociologists, curators. This publication is a good example of what they consider architecture should be, a discipline that listens, pulls down borders and boundaries, and initiates a dialogue – a different form of building.

Valence

Ho Chi Minh City

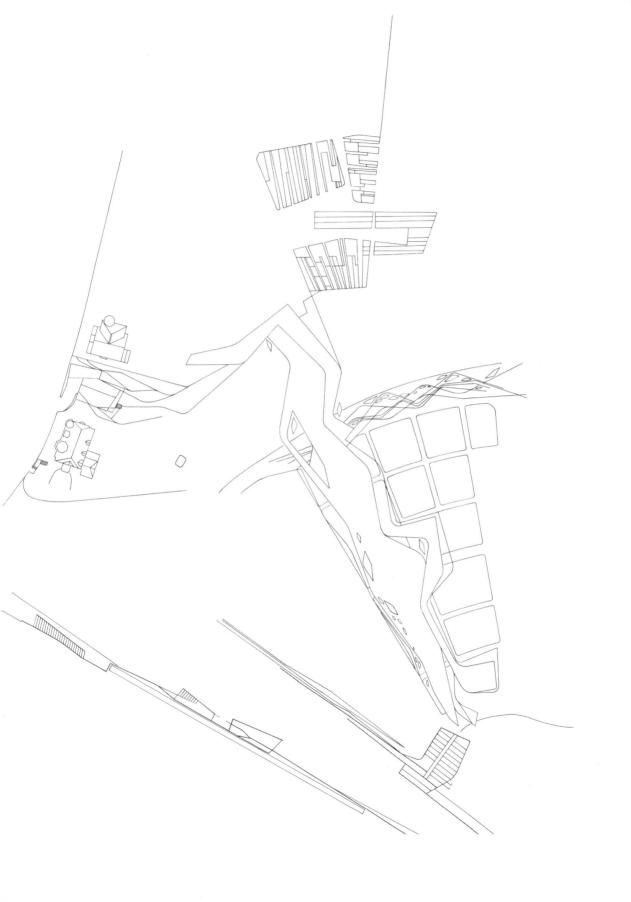

MARCUS ALTFELD is Professor of Medicine at Harvard Medical School, and Director of the Innate Immunity Program at the Ragon Institute of MGH, MIT and Harvard. He also serves as an Honorary Professor at the University of KwaZulu-Natal in Durban, South Africa and as a Visiting Professor at the 4th Military Medical School in Xi'an, China. Professor Altfeld studies the responses of the immune system against HIV-1, with the aim of contributing to the development of an HIV Vaccine.

VICTORIA BELL is an artist. She studied painting at the University of California, Berkeley and has exhibited internationally. Selected one-person shows include: 2011, LVR-LandesMuseum, Bonn; 1986–2009, Galerie Carla Stützer, Cologne; 2004, Lemmons Contemporary, New York; 2003, Flottmann-Hallen, Herne, BRD; 1996, Rhona Hoffman Gallery (Gallery 312), Chicago. Selected group shows: 2011–12, Kolumba, Cologne; 2002, „Köln-Skulptur", ART COLOGNE, Linda Durham Contemporary Art, Galisteo, New York.
Her work is also exhibited in various public collections, including: Kolumba, Cologne; LVR-LandesMuseum, Bonn; Museum Ludwig, Cologne; the Cities of Wesel, Chicago, Duisburg-Rheinhausen.

AARON BETSKY is Director of the Cincinnati Art Museum. In 2008, he directed the 11th International Architecture Biennale Venice. Trained as an architect, Mr. Betsky is a critic, teacher, and writer whose work has been extensively published. He started his career working as a designer for Frank Gehry and teaching at the Southern California Institute of Architecture (SCI-Arc). From 1995 to 2001, he was Curator of Architecture, Design, and Digital Projects at the San Francisco Museum of Modern Art, and from 2001 to 2006 he was Director of the Netherlands Architecture Institute in Rotterdam. His collected essays, *At Home in Sprawl*, was published by RMIT Press in 2011.

WILHELM BRUCK, born 1943 in Germany. Growing up "in the 19th century", in a Bavarian village - without church, school, shops, motor-vehicles, or music heard on loudspeakers - influenced his acoustic sense. He studied music (guitar and lute) in Cologne during the sixties. Fascinated by the development of the New Music in these years - which was dominated by Stockhausen, Kagel and B.A. Zimmermann, as well as the FLUXUS movement - he soon became a member of that scene, working and touring with Kagel's "Kölner Ensemble für Neue Musik". In 1972 he founded the "Duo Bruck-Ross", with Theodor Ross, developing a concert programme which was distinguished by the consistent combination of music and performance. Together they also premiered, among others, Kagel's *Zwei-Mann-Orchester* and Lachenmann's *Salut für Caudwell*. From 1980-1990 he held a professorship for guitar at the Musikhochschule Karlsruhe. His interest in new forms of expression for the guitar has inspired many composers. He now runs international courses and master classes for guitar and instrumental theatre.

RICKY BURDETT is Professor of Urban Studies at the London School of Economics, Director of LSE Cities and co-editor, with Deyan Sudjic, of *Living in the Endless City*, published by Phaidon. He was director of the 2006 Venice Architecture Biennale and curator of the *Global Cities* exhibition at Tate Modern.

BEATRICE GALILEE is a London-based curator, writer, critic and lecturer in contemporary architecture and design. She is the Chief Curator of the 2013 Lisbon Architecture Triennale, co-founder and director of The Gopher Hole, an experimental exhibition and event space in London, architectural consultant and writer at DomusWeb and Associate Lecturer at Central St Martins. She worked as a curator at the 2011 Gwangju Design Biennale and 2009 Shenzhen Hong Kong Biennale. She is the former architecture editor of *Icon* magazine, where she won the architecture journalist of the year award, and is a freelance contributor and critic to a number of publications on architecture and design.

MICHAEL JANSEN was Director Research Program (DFG) Mohenjo-Daro, Pakistan, 1979-87.
Since 1988 he has been Professor (History of Urbanisation) at RWTH, Aachen.
Guest Professor at Nagoya Institute of Technology, Japan; Leuven University, Belgium; Harvard University, USA; Sultan Qaboos University, Oman; GUTech Uiversity Oman.
Senior Advisor and Consultant UNESCO, ICOMOS, Paris; Ministry of Culture, Oman; Ministry of Awqaf, Oman; UNESCO Projects in Afghanistan (Bamiyan, Herat), Kazakhstan, Kyrgyzstan, Pakistan, India, Oman.
He is the author of four books and more than 70 publications.

RITA KERSTING is an art historian living in Nijmegen, The Netherlands.
She was Director of Kunstverein für die Rheinlande und Westfalen, Düsseldorf, 2001-07
and now works as a freelance curator and writer. Recent work includes shows and texts on Özlem Altin, Len Lye, Ruth Laskey and Serge Alain Nitegeka

JAN-MAURITS LOECKE is an architect and author living in London.
Founding partner of He.Lo Architects, 2002. Studied Architecture at ETSA Sevilla and RWTH Aachen, where he graduated in 1999. Surrounded by art and music he started his journey in his hometown Cologne. He worked with Jean Nouvel in Paris and with Alfredo Arribas and Enric Miralles + Benedetta Tagliabue in Barcelona, where he met Sónia Nunes Henriques. During his London years he was first with Farrells and then RTKL working on projects in the Middle East and China. He has been involved in research projects in Ladakh and Kashmir (DFG Berlin and Jan Pieper) and was a guest critic at the Architectural Association, 2006-2010.

OSCAR RIBEIRO DE ALMEIDA NIEMEYER SOARES FILHO established himself in the 1940s, 50s and 60s as one of Modernism's greatest luminaries, reshaping Brazil's identity in the popular imagination and mesmerizing architects around the globe. Oscar Niemeyer's contribution to architecture in Brazil and throughout the world is immense with a professional life spanning almost a century. He designed many iconic buildings mostly characterized by his revolutionary and daring use of concrete, pioneering the exploration of the formal possibilities of reinforced concrete solely for their aesthetic impact. He is currently 104 years old and still working.

PAULO SERGIO NIEMEYER, was born into a family of architects. He studied in Sao Bras University in Sao Paulo, Brazil, graduating in 1999. He worked with Walter Makhohl at Makhohl Arquitectura where he became a partner in 2000. Paulo Sergio currently runs his own office, Niemeyer Associados, in Rio de Janeiro and collaborates with his great-grandfather Oscar Niemeyer.

SONIA NUNES HENRIQUES is a London-based architect, a founding partner of He.Lo Architects in 2002. She graduated from Lisbon Technical University in 1999. She has worked in Barcelona with Enric Miralles + Benedetta Tagliabue and in London with John McAslan + Partners. She has been involved in projects such as the Scottish Parliament, Edinburgh, with EMBT, and the Iron Market, Haiti, with John McAslan + Partners.

HANS ULRICH OBRIST is Co-director of the Serpentine Gallery in London. Prior to this, he was Curator of the Musée d'Art Moderne de la Ville de Paris. He has co-curated over 250 exhibitions since his first exhibition, *The Kitchen Show (World Soup)* in 1991. He has contributed to over 200 book projects; his recent publications include *A Brief History of Curating*, Project Japan: Metabolism Talks with Rem Koolhaas, *Ai Wei Wei Speaks*, along with two volumes of his selected interviews. In 2011, Obrist was awarded both the Bard College Award for Curatorial Excellence and the Swiss Institute Honoree Award.

R.B. PARKINSON was trained at Oxford, and after a junior research fellowship there, he joined the Department of Ancient Egypt and Sudan at the British Museum, where he has worked ever since. He continues to teach and to supervise students internationally. Curatorial projects have included the display of the Rosetta Stone, a gallery on Ancient Egyptian Life and Death including the Nebamun wall-paintings, and the Ramesseum Papyri. His research interests centre around literary theory, and he is widely regarded as an international authority on Ancient Egyptian poetry of the golden age.

SASKIA SASSEN is the Robert S. Lynd Professor of Sociology and Co-Chair, The Committee on Global Thought, Columbia University. Her recent books are *Territory, Authority, Rights: From Medieval to Global Assemblages* (Princeton University Press, 2008), *A Sociology of Globalization* (W.W. Norton 2007), and the 4th fully updated edition of *Cities in a World Economy* (Sage 2012). Among older books is *The Global City* (Princeton University Press 1991/2001). Her books are translated into over 20 languages. She is the recipient of diverse awards and mentions, ranging from multiple doctor *honoris causa* to named lectures and being selected as one of the 100 Top Global Thinkers of 2011 by *Foreign Policy Magazine*. www.saskiasassen.com

ÁLVARO JOAQUIM MELO SIZA VIEIRA studied at the School of Architecture, University of Porto, 1949-55. He taught at the School of Architecture (ESBAP) from l966-69 and was appointed Professor of "Construction" in 1976. He is a member of the American Academy of Arts and Science, Honorary Fellow of the Royal Institute of British Architects, AIA/American Institute of Architects, Académie d'Architecture de France, the European Academy of Sciences and Arts, and the American Academy of Arts and Letters.

HILDEGARD WEBER is an artist living in Cologne. Her work and interactive media installations are distinguished by their critical theory and philosophy, their openness, psychological complexity and profound humour. Conflicts of fragments are one aspect of her visual sequences as are experiments with sound, video, photo, music and language. She exhibits projects and has taught photography. She was *Artiste Invitée* at the Ecole des Beaux Arts. Dijon. Her installations are dialogues - unrivalled in their relevance to current events and issues of "expanded art".

BRIAN SHEFTON born in Cologne in 1919 and sadly passed away in Newcastle on 27 January 2012.
As he was invited to contribute to *Spatial Murmuring* we would like to use this space to commemorate Brian and to pay respect to his extraordinary life and work. He was a distinguished scholar of Greek and Etruscan archaeology. One of his most significant achievements was a collection of Greek and Etruscan artefacts, which he established in 1956. The collection expanded to include nearly 1,000 objects, many of which can now be seen at the Great North Museum: Hancock, in Newcastle upon Tyne designed by Terry Farrell. His scholarship was truly international. He attended international conferences frequently, and also received prestigious fellowships and honours, including an honorary doctorate from Cologne University and the British Academy's Kenyon medal. He is survived by his wife Jutta and his daughter.